A FIRST LOOK AT AMERICA'S PRESIDENTS

JOHN ADAMS

The 2nd President

by Josh Gregory

Consultant: Meena Bose
Director, Peter S. Kalikow Center for the Study of the American Presidency
Peter S. Kalikow Chair in Presidential Studies
Professor, Political Science
Hofstra University
Hempstead, New York

BEARPORT
PUBLISHING

New York, New York

Credits

Cover, © Alliance Images/Alamy; 4, © North Wind Picture Archives/Alamy; 5L, United States Navy; 5R, © mattesimages/
Shutterstock.com; 6, © The Design Lab; 7, Courtesy of the Daderot/commons.wikimedia.org/CC BY-SA 3.0; 8, © Bettmann/
Corbis/AP Images; 9T, Courtesy of the Architect of the Capitol; 9B, © Susan Law Cain/Shutterstock.com; 10, Courtesy of
the Library of Congress; 11, © North Wind Picture Archives/Alamy; 12, © Stocktrek Images, Inc./Alamy; 13T, © North
Wind Picture Archives/Alamy; 13B, © Vlad G/Shutterstock.com; 14, Courtesy of the Library of Congress; 15, © Glasshouse
Images/Alamy; 16, Courtesy of the Library of Congress; 17, © Vacclav/Shutterstock.com; 18, © National Gallery of Art/
Alamy; 19T, Courtesy of the Library of Congress; 19B, Courtesy of the Library of Congress; 20L, © North Wind Picture
Archives/Alamy; 20R, © Susan Law Cain/Shutterstock.com; 21TL, © North Wind Picture Archives/Alamy; 21TR, Courtesy of
the United States Navy; 21B, Courtesy of the Library of Congress; 22, © spirit of america/Shutterstock.com; 23T, © Vlad G/
Shutterstock.com; 23B, © Susan Law Cain/Shutterstock.com.

Publisher: Kenn Goin
Editor: Joyce Tavolacci
Creative Director: Spencer Brinker
Design: The Design Lab
Photo Researcher: Josh Gregory

Special thanks to fifth-grader Lucy Barr and second-grader Brian Barr for their help in reviewing this book.

Library of Congress Cataloging-in-Publication Data

Gregory, Josh.
 John Adams: the 2nd President / by Josh Gregory ; consultant, Meena Bose, Director, Peter S. Kalikow Center for the Study
of the American Presidency, Peter S. Kalikow Chair in Presidential Studies, Professor, political science, Hofstra University,
Hempstead, New York.
     pages cm. — (A first look at America's Presidents)
 Includes bibliographical references and index.
 ISBN 978-1-62724-558-6 (library binding) – ISBN 1-62724-558-8 (library binding)
 1. Adams, John, 1735–1826–Juvenile literature. 2. Presidents–United States–Biography–Juvenile literature. I. Bose,
Meenekshi, 1970– II. Title. III. Title: John Adams, the second President.
 E322.G75 2015
 973.4'4092–dc23
 [B]
                                        2014034555

For more information, write to Bearport Publishing Company, Inc., 45 West 21st Street, Suite 3B,
New York, New York 10010. Printed in the United States of America.

10 9 8 7 6 5 4 3 2 1

CONTENTS

Standing Up for Freedom

John Adams boldly spoke out for freedom. At one time, Great Britain ruled America. Adams helped Americans end British rule and form their own government. Then, as president, Adams led the brand-new nation.

Americans fought a war to end British rule.

John Adams was the second president. He served from 1797 to 1801.

Adams strongly believed that Americans should be able to choose their own government.

Born in the Colonies

John Adams was born in 1735. His family lived on a farm in the **colony** of Massachusetts. John was a good student. He grew up to be a lawyer.

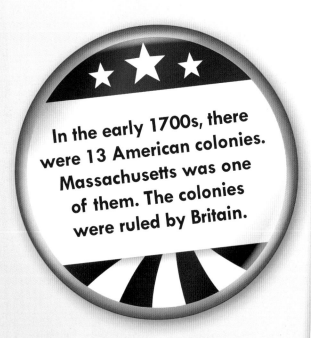

In the early 1700s, there were 13 American colonies. Massachusetts was one of them. The colonies were ruled by Britain.

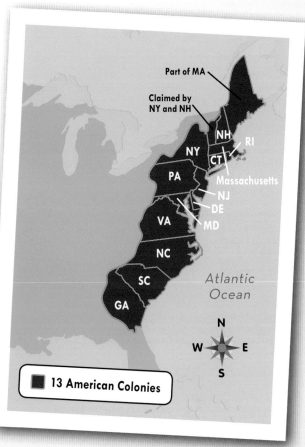

Part of MA

Claimed by NY and NH

NH

RI

NY

CT

PA

Massachusetts

NJ

DE

VA

MD

NC

SC

GA

Atlantic Ocean

N

W   E

S

■ 13 American Colonies

John Adams was born in this farmhouse in what is now Quincy, Massachusetts.

Speaking Out

In the 1760s, the colonies paid many **taxes** to Britain. Adams thought the taxes were unfair. He wrote and spoke against them. Then, in 1776, Adams helped write an important **text**. It said that America should be free from British rule. The text was the **Declaration of Independence**.

This is a copy of the Declaration of Independence.

Adams

Adams was one of five men who helped write the Declaration of Independence.

Abigail Adams

Adams married Abigail Smith in 1764. Abigail had many ideas about what Americans should do. She often gave John advice.

9

War Breaks Out

Britain did not want to give up its American colonies. To win their freedom, Americans went to war. In 1783, they won the fight. A group of leaders signed a peace **treaty** with Britain. Adams was one of them.

The war was called the Revolutionary War.

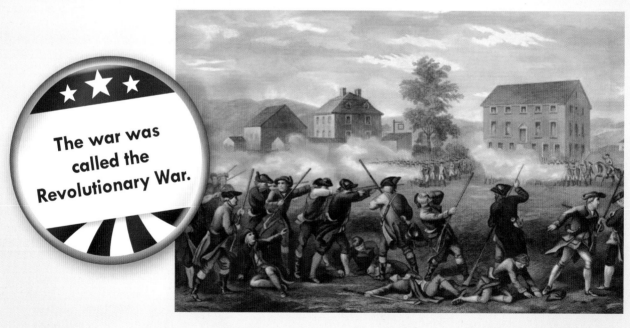

The first battle of the war was fought in 1775. After the Declaration of Independence was signed, more Americans joined the fight.

The Revolutionary War ended after British troops surrendered, or gave up, to American troops.

Vice President

The United States was free. Now the new nation needed leaders. George Washington became the first president in 1789. John Adams was the first vice president. With Abigail, he moved to New York City. This was the nation's first **capital**.

Before becoming president, George Washington had led American troops during the Revolutionary War.

As vice president, Adams helped shape the nation's government during its early years.

Adams

In 1790, Philadelph[ia] became the country['s] second capital. John [and] Abigail moved agai[n].

Independence Hall in Philadelphia

President

In 1796, Adams was **elected** president. At the time, Britain and France were at war. They sometimes attacked U.S. ships. Adams started the U.S. Navy to protect the ships.

The U.S.S. *United States* (right) was one of the ships built for the U.S. Navy during Adams's presidency.

Adams knew a strong navy was important to protect the United States.

Adams is sometimes called the Father of the Navy.

The New Capital

In 1800, Washington, D.C., became the country's new capital. A new house for the president was being built there. It was later called the White House. Adams moved in before it was finished.

Adams was the first president to live in the White House.

This is how the White House looked in about 1800.

The White House today

Remembering Adams

John Adams believed in America. He helped free the colonies from British rule. He also helped shape the new country. For these reasons, Adams is known as one of the Founding Fathers.

After leaving office, Adams spent time with Abigail and the rest of his family in Massachusetts.

Adams

This building, which is part of the Library of Congress in Washington, D.C., is named after Adams. It's called the John Adams Building.

Adams died on July 4, 1826. This was exactly 50 years after the Declaration of Independence was written and signed.

Here are some major events from John Adams's life.

1776
Adams and other leaders write and sign the Declaration of Independence.

1735
John Adams is born in the colony of Massachusetts.

1730

1770

1780

1775
The Revolutionary War begins.

1783
The United States wins th Revolutionary War.

1796
Adams is elected as the nation's second president.

1790

1800

1830

1789
Adams becomes the first vice president of the United States.

1826
Adams dies on July 4 at his home in Quincy, Massachusetts.

FACTS and QUOTES

"Let us dare to read, think, speak, and write."

When apart, John and Abigail Adams wrote each other letters almost every day.

John and Abigail Adams had six children. One of them, John Quincy Adams, became the 6th president of the United States.

"Children should be educated and instructed in the principles of freedom."

"Liberty, once lost, is lost forever."

John Adams

GLOSSARY

capital (KAP-uh-tuhl) a city where a country's government is based

colony (KOL-uh-nee) a place that has been settled by people from another country and is ruled by that country

Declaration of Independence (dek-luh-RAY-shuhn UV in-di-PEN-duhnss) a text signed by American leaders on July 4, 1776, that declared the freedom of the 13 American colonies from British rule

elected (i-LEK-tihd) chosen by voting to hold a public office

taxes (TAKS-iz) money paid by people to the ruler or government of a country

text (TEKST) a written work

treaty (TREE-tee) a written agreement between countries

23

Index

Read More

Harness, Cheryl. *The Revolutionary John Adams*. Washington, DC: National Geographic (2003).

Hopkinson, Deborah. *John Adams Speaks for Freedom (Stories of Famous Americans)*. New York: Aladdin Library (2005).

Learn More Online

To learn more about John Adams, visit **www.bearportpublishing.com/AmericasPresidents**

About the Author: Josh Gregory writes and edits books for kids. He lives in Chicago, Illinois.